THE DEATH OF SUCCESS

A wide-ranging true story of one of the most influential of all professions, never before told and built around the collapse of a shining star in the world of marketing. It should not have happened.

A Personal Memoir and Useful Business Guide by

ALLEN STONE

Broadcast Journalist. Senior Advertising Executive.

DEDICATION

For Jim, Scott, Maria, Elliot, Rosann, Peter, Mike, and all the others who made me look so good for so long.

This book is dedicated to the talented creative professionals I was privileged to supervise for more than 16 halcyon years. My life could never have been as challenging, as fulfilling—or as much fun—without them.

The song goes something like: "there's no business like show business, and no people like show people." Allow me to make those words read: "there's no business more torturing than advertising, and no people more willing to be tortured than advertising people."

CONTENTS

Introduction 7

Chapter 1: Nothing Will Change 11
 Live through that fateful Saturday morning in early October
 when everything changed.

Chapter 2: Never the Kremlin 16
 Experience the pain and suffering of a punishing corporate
 environment.

Chapter 3: Writing A Great Creative Brief 26
 Learn how the absence of solid marketing can compromise the
 strength of the creative work.

Chapter 4: The Management Meetings 33
 Be a fly on the wall at these unproductive talkfests, rife with
 posturing rather than problem-solving.

Chapter 5: Communication & Teamwork 43
 Make an assault on the lost art of communication, applicable to
 any business or industry.

Chapter 6: The Staff Endured 55
 Marvel at employee resiliency, despite wounds that would never
 heal and decisions that were out of character.

Chapter 7: Bob Schmetterer, The B.M.O.C. of Advertising 58
 Meet the advertising icon forced into retirement as he charted
 a course he claimed would transform the nature of business
 itself.

Chapter 8: Dismantling the Bureaucracy **64**

Witness how a CEO can lose his grip on reality and turn away from his most trusted managers.

Chapter 9: Faster, Better, Cheaper **70**

Find out how this client-induced mandate creates barriers to the development of quality advertising and plays havoc with agency profits.

Chapter 10: Changing Colors **75**

See how black ink can turn red and put top professionals out on the street after years of sweating blood for the company store.

Chapter 11: Talent for the Times **80**

Imagine losing the brainpower of long-sought-after "new breed" designers and writers who made their agency a leader in Internet advertising.

Epilogue: Facing the Facts **87**

Shadows of the past . . . heralds of the future . . . and a personal postscript.

INTRODUCTION

This is an advertising story within a story. It exposes practices never before brought into an open forum, and issues unknown outside this industry that has shaped our purchasing patterns and seduced us with its powers of persuasion. It is built around the demise of Devon Direct, the largest Direct Response advertising agency in the Euro RSCG Worldwide marketing combine . . . a network of close to 200 agencies in 72 countries. Euro RSCG—a merger in 1991 of Eurocom with Roux, Seguela, Caysac and Goudard—is a division of Paris-based Havas, one of the world's preeminent communication conglomerates.

Devon Direct was a top-ten direct marketer headquartered in suburban Philadelphia, with offices throughout the U.S. as well as overseas, and representing a diverse range of Fortune 500 clients. Its downfall is a microcosm of everything that can bring a proud and productive agency from an exalted position to the edge of disaster. While shedding new light on the character and inner workings of the advertising profession, this book tells the troubling story of a company that grew from humble beginnings to the stature of a top-rung ad agency. It is a chronicle of success gone sour . . . of leadership that lost its ability to lead, of pressures that often depressed the human spirit, of ill-conceived business directions and the near destruction of all that is sacred in advertising: Ideas. Innovation. Motivation. Willingness to abide client excess. Determination to meet stringent timeframes. Tolerance for working unconscionable hours. Even relegating family subservient to the workplace.

You capitulate to this reality without compromise if you're excited, rewarded and convinced that you're in the right place, with the right people, working in an unequalled environment of creative freedom . . . and serving blue chip clients that feed the agency's as well as your own ability to grow and prosper.

When those nourishing conditions cease to exist, it's a barren landscape in which you're sapped of your energy, your confidence in the company, and worst of all—your ability to find within yourself the depth of expression and idea generation necessary to create the most impactful advertising. You are face-to-face with the death of success.

This factual account of the agency that dominated the Philadelphia advertising scene and extended its reach into the national and international marketplace will strike a responsive chord with all those whose positions at that agency were diminished . . . with all who toil under the crushing demands of an advertising career . . . and with all who would be fascinated by the first-ever look inside Direct Response, the fastest growing and most unique channel of offline/online marketing. It reveals, for the first time, policies and behavioral patterns in the advertising world that are disturbing to agency/client interaction and demoralizing to the devoted people who labor in the trenches. I'll introduce you to many of these dedicated professionals—to what they do and how they do it, often under burdens that are less than desirable. And often at the behest of leaders who, in my view, failed them.

You will be an insider to what life is really like in an ad agency . . . including a first-hand look at actual processes that give form and substance to creative development. The words will conjure images much as they do in a best-selling fictional novel. As you turn the pages, you'll recall those TV sitcoms—Bosom Buddies, Bewitched and Melrose Place—that made advertising seem so glamorous. What goes on between agencies and clients will surprise you. And my promise is that you will not find a book on advertising as entertaining, as revealing or as interesting a learning experience.

What's more, for any business person or committed professional, this book is particularly important reading. It is an instructive lesson in corporate failure, applicable to virtually any company that loses its way, alienates its employees and offers no hope of a secure future.

The Death Of Success is a real story about real people, little known and well-known. This is the way I saw it . . . and lived it. These are my opinions, as a key member of the Devon Direct management.

CHAPTER I

NOTHING WILL CHANGE

The phone rang in our 8th floor condominium on Presidential Boulevard in the Philadelphia suburb of Bala Cynwyd—the most mispronounced name of any town in the region. (phonetically Kinwid, not Sinwid.) It was a sun-drenched Saturday morning in early October of 1999. Clothing and suitcases were strewn throughout the den/ computer room in preparation for our Sunday departure to Paris.

Jill and I were in the sixth year of our marriage, the second for both of us. Although beyond the usual retirement age, we remained vibrantly healthy and fully occupied with our individual pursuits. Jill held the prestigious position of docent at the world class Philadelphia Museum of Art. I was continuing a productive career as Vice President/Creative Director of Devon Direct Marketing & Advertising. At that point, we were the eighth largest Direct Response agency in the United States, the largest agency of any kind in the Philadelphia region and growing at an annual rate of 20 percent. We were serving an enviable list of important clients at home and abroad, including such telecommunication giants as Sprint, MCI, Bell Atlantic (now Verizon) and British Telecom. Our mission being to provide these and other industry-leading corporations with through-the-mail and online business-to-business and business-to-consumer advertising.

Direct Marketing had come of age. It was mainstream, no longer "junk mail" in the eyes of the advertising profession nor the millions of businesses and consumers who were responding to its targeted messages. Its rise was meteoric and our skilled professionals were pacesetters. They had pushed the limits of this unique one-on-one medium beyond conventional boundaries—turning many of America's biggest and most powerful companies into Direct Response believers, creating new links to their prospects, widening their customer bases and enhancing their revenues. Our DM packages contained a clarity and style that set us apart. We had established a reputation for refining Direct Response applications and maximizing potential . . . not only through product and service advertising, direct mail customer retention campaigns, and customer winback programs, but by mastering such new and fertile areas as image, awareness, informational and educational campaigns.

We invented and marketed the Sprint FŌNCARD^{SM}, created the first-of-its-kind program utilized by MCI to win subscribers on a neighborhood by neighborhood basis, developed GMAC Home Solutions, a new sub-brand unifying all third party products and services under the GMAC umbrella, upgraded the entire public perception of stodgy, customer insensitive British Telecom . . . and served a diverse range of growth-oriented companies—from ADT Security Systems, Fleet financial services, *Commentary* magazine, and Nextel wireless communications to IBM, Wyeth-Lederle, Nutri System weight loss centers and J.I. Case farm/construction equipment.

In addition, we united the forces of marketing and technology, pioneering the use of such production techniques as personalization and customization. These processes strengthened Direct Marketing's ability to target an audience most likely to buy a product and continually measure the results through the inclusion of response-tracking mechanisms. Thus offering clients the only truly accountable form of advertising from a return-on-investment perspective.

Our annual commitment of more than 300 to 400 million pieces of direct mail was an industry benchmark and our digital division ranked among the top 50 interactive agencies in North America. In fact, we were a leader in the development of Web-based advertising.

All was well in the fall of 1999—the agency's16th year in business, my12th year with the company—and there was no indication that would change. Still, I had become troubled by certain, almost imperceptible, cracks in the armor of the agency, in its culture and in its capacity for garnering new business. True, we were an award winner, widely recognized as a powerhouse in worldwide Direct Marketing, with annual double-digit growth spawning billings in the stratosphere and blue-chip clients we could brag about. Yet, something was not right. Directions were being embraced and decisions made that would, in time, alter our course and reinvent our future.

It was Ron Greene—President, CEO, founder and owner of Devon Direct—on the phone that October day. "Hi Allen, Ron here. Hate to intrude on your Saturday morning. I know you're getting ready to leave for a Paris vacation, but I have to talk with you. Can I come to your apartment?"

"Sure Ron, what's going on?"

"It's something you have to know before you leave. I don't want you to come back and find out after I announce it to the agency next week."

"Okay Ron, see you soon."

Ron and I had been a winning team. We believed in each other. I will never forget the pride I felt when, at my 10th anniversary party, he told the assembled employees that he could not have built the agency without me. There were also the times he would say, "you'll go down with the ship." A metaphor that would turn into a prophesy.

Despite our close professional alliance, there was no social relationship. I had calculatedly avoided that, preferring to work every day at being a superior administrator, to give something back to this man who had given me so much encouragement, not to speak of the challenges and rewards coveted by every professional.

"Hi Ron, c'mon in."

Tall, tanned, athletic, with deep brown gentle eyes, Ron Greene always spoke in the language of a gentleman. By nature an entrepreneur, he had the ability to spot at a glance the strengths and weaknesses of a piece of advertising. Tough and demanding, at the same time gracious and fun loving, his greatest pleasure was to shirtsleeve it with his creative people, to understand their problems and contribute his own valuable insights to their efforts. Unfortunately, the day would come when that would change, when Ron would closet himself in his office, isolate himself from his most trusted managers, ignore their recommendations and create a cocoon of protection from the harsh realities of an impending disaster.

"Can I get you a cup of coffee Ron?"

"No thanks. Boy, this is a beautiful apartment!"

"Thank you, we're happy here. Jill is out tying up some loose ends before we leave tomorrow. What's up?"

Ron fidgeted, uneasy with what he was about to say. "Allen, I've sold the company. But I'm here to tell you that I'm staying as President and CEO and I need you to stay with me. Nothing will change. We will keep our identity. Our people will continue to prosper. And this move will help us grow our business because we will become part of Euro RSCG, a division of the French communications conglomerate Havas. Euro controls nearly 200 prominent and successful ad agencies throughout the world. With that kind of power, how can it be anything but good for Devon Direct?"

I quickly assembled my thoughts, wanting to respond as positively as I could. "I'm not surprised Ron. It's the right time for you to do this, for yourself and for all of us who are devoted to keeping our company on the high road." As Ron continued to talk of the future, I mused to myself . . . asking why, when companies are bought and sold, do they always say nothing will change. It most usually does, and it did.

I thought to myself, I would deal with it when Jill and I get back from Paris.

CHAPTER 2

NEVER THE KREMLIN

I first met Ron Greene at the Franklin Mint where he was a Vice President. Before that he occupied the position of General Manager at *Commentary* magazine. I arrived at the Mint following a long and exhilarating career in Philadelphia as a broadcast journalist with Walter Annenberg's Triangle Publications Radio and Television Division. A career that began at radio station WTTM, a one-time major communications outlet in Trenton, New Jersey where I was a staff announcer along with Ernie Kovacs and Jack Barry. Jack—cocky and self-assured—went to New York, had a facial makeover and gained fame as the handsome quizmaster whose rigged TV show "Twenty-One" led to the infamous scandal depicted in the Robert Redford film "Quiz Show." Jack's life was cut short when he was fatally stricken while jogging in Central Park. Ernie went to Philadelphia, then on to Hollywood where he became a star in movies and on the Steve Allen television show, only to lose his life in a tragic automobile accident on the West Coast in January of 1962. He was as neat a guy and as clever a comic as I've ever known.

I picked up a degree at the University of Pennsylvania and made my mark as a newscaster and analyst at WFIL radio and television, the

Philadelphia broadcast properties that launched the careers of my two buddies from earlier days—Eddie Fisher and Dick Clark. Eddie was as high on talent as he was in pursuit of beautiful women. And we all know where that got him. Though talent was not his strongest suit, Dick was high on brainpower. And we all know where that got *him*. I remember the day Dick, an obscure radio disc jockey, was assigned to front the Bandstand program. His income shot up from hundreds to thousands of dollars a week and he took himself to the top of the charts as a pop music icon.

When my broadcast career subsided, I put my writing skills to work at the Franklin Mint, the Direct Marketing giant founded in 1964 as a maker of coins by the legendary Joseph Segel—an entrepreneur of enormous vision. However, there was not a day in my five years at the Mint that I did not see myself as trapped in a cauldron of intimidation. Such was my perception of the environment at the Franklin Mint. To make matters worse, I knew nothing about Direct Response advertising. But I quickly realized that the Mint was a repository of creative genius, promoting its collectibles to loyal customers throughout the world through ingenious marketing tactics.

To lend legitimacy and an aura of importance to its thousands of products—many sourced in the Far East to take advantage of unique skills and cheap labor—the Mint regularly engaged in compensated arrangements with prestigious institutions around the globe. They became "official" sponsors of its collections, sculptures, dolls, jewelry and other works of art. Examples:

The 1930 Duesenberg J Derham Tourster—a precision model officially authorized by the Heritage Plantation of Sandwich Antique Automobile Museum.

Pheasant of The Springtime Blossoms—hand-painted on pure silk and issued by The Shanghai Museum of China.

The Great Battles of The Civil War Sculpture Collection—an official issue of The National Historical Society.

The Cavalryman—a cold-cast bronze sculpture commissioned by The Western Heritage Museum.

The Mint's marketing strategy was to convince prospective purchasers that they would not only receive personal pleasure from owning what has been referred to as "tchotchkes," (phonetically chochkis) but be admired for their discriminating taste in acquiring collectibles that would draw the attention of all who see them. And that these "limited editions" would become sought-after heirlooms, thus appreciating in value. The latter eventually was shot down by the government as a no-no. Which by no means suggests that these products were not of the highest quality or worth the purchase price.

The Mint was its own client and agency, staffed by an impressive assembly of Direct Marketing specialists. There was much to learn and I learned it well, thanks largely to people like Ron Greene and my boss Ed Trautman . . . a man of uncommon wisdom who saw in me what I did not see in myself. He gave me the strength to not only survive the rigors of the Mint, but to carve out a reputation as one of his most valued promotional writers.

When the Resnicks bought the Mint from Warner Communications and dumped the ruling hierarchy, I was uncomfortable with this new ownership. The feeling at the Mint, true or not, was that Lynda and Stewart Resnick had little interest in the importance of the creative people and felt they were overpaid. Ron Greene had already departed to launch Devon Direct Marketing and Advertising in partnership with a colleague at the Mint—the brainy, enigmatic James Perry, a marketer with abundant experience in high-level corporate positions. Unlike Ron Greene, it was not easy to know Jim Perry unless he respected you. I would later on learn that Jim preferred to operate quietly in the background, guarding agency finances, while leaving Ron in the foreground as company front man and chief creative officer. During our years together at Devon Direct, I had no problems with Jim. We enjoyed our interaction immensely, delighted in picking each other's brains and benefited from each other's capabilities.

My mentor at the Mint, Ed Trautman, had fallen into the clutches of the ambitious Nita Martin who got in with the Resnicks, engineered his downgrading and took over the copy department. Under pressure from Nita because of my loyalty to Ed Trautman, I departed the Mint in February of 1987. Hearing of my availability, Ron and Jim quickly brought me into their agency, first as Copy Chief and shortly thereafter, Vice President/Creative Director.

Nita Martin eventually lost her luster at the Mint and was shown the door. She indicated an interest in coming to Devon Direct, even cornered me at a party, told me I was her big mistake, and then approached Jim Perry to ask if it would be possible for her to take up a role at Devon. Jim referred her to me but I did not respond. I think they call that divine retribution.

To this day, I refer to my years at the Franklin Mint as the worst five years of my professional life and the best five years of my professional life. The worst because they were a baptism in fire, the best because I landed upright and nailed down a new career. My most unnerving memory of those five years? I have never before and never since known any terror equal to facing the dynasty of Mint moguls around the conference room table. It was akin to an inquisition. They seemed to take fiendish delight in reducing you to ruin when passing judgement on your work. On the other hand, you won their respect if you could withstand the shocks and tough it out.

Meanwhile, the once great Franklin Mint, at last report, was hitting the skids. Its dependable market was maturing and replacement collectors were increasingly hard to come by. But that's a "death-of-success" story worthy of another book.

Early on at Devon, walking the corridor with Ron, he made me a promise. "Allen, I will never allow this agency to become the Kremlin," his characterization of the Franklin Mint. For a time, he was true to his word. The creative freedom he encouraged and his respect for talent were the underpinnings of a culture that attracted advertising's most innovative professionals. It was an enviable culture within which our people prospered. Their careers advanced, their compensation kept pace with their accomplishments and we garnered the most prestigious awards in the advertising industry.

I built a department of skilled writers and influenced a corps of exceptional designers. I added administrative strength to my creative capabilities. Each day brought me the challenges and rewards every professional craves. I was king of the creative heap at a premier Direct Marketing agency that was scoring one success after another, winning major clients one after another.

Lest you get the impression that all this was happening with equanimity, not so. Sprint had us on the run keeping up with their demands. When we left Sprint and took on MCI, the pressure to satisfy this client was deafening. I recall the year, just before the Labor Day weekend, when MCI suddenly came up with a list of assignments requiring immediate attention. When told that the agency would be closed for the holiday weekend with all employees off, MCI said guess what, your people will be working the weekend, holiday or not.

Another woeful MCI story comes to mind. It was the day of a terrible snowstorm. MCI asked the agency to courier a parcel of advertising materials down to Washington. Ron Greene said, no way. He would not subject anyone to such a hazard. Asked where the materials needed to go, MCI said direct to the home of one of its marketers who had no intention of going to work in the snow.

You didn't work *with* MCI, you worked *for* MCI. The poor account executives at Devon Direct that had to interact with MCI dropped like flies.

This kind of demeaning client behavior is not unusual in advertising. Agencies and their clients are often confrontational and it's the agencies that have no choice but to throw in the towel. The harsh reality is either acquiesce to client demands or lose the business. With no other option, agencies are forced to push their people into grinding out advertising that plays havoc with creativity and threatens burnout. In addition to MCI, we were a vassal to Bell Atlantic, ADT Security Systems, British Telecom, Fleet Bank and for that matter, virtually all other clients. Agencies accept these client-imposed conditions as normal. It's the price of profit.

There is an aspect of overbearing client behavior that deserves elaboration. It undermines an agency's capacity for delivering the best work and intensifies the adversarial relationship between agency and client.

The client orders work. The client dictates the schedule for completion of the advertising and entering it into the marketplace. The agency launches the process, discovers the need for further information from the client on a rushed basis so creative development can move forward. The client is in no hurry to respond.

This problem persists through the process. The agency finishes the work, presents it to the client. The client again delays getting back, then orders a raft of changes. The revisions are implemented and the work is returned to the client, along with the agency's request that it be given immediate attention for the sake of holding to the schedule.

The client continues its heedless attitude while refusing to alter the schedule. Finally, the work reaches the finish line . . . sometimes blowing the budget, which in itself causes friction and adds to the agency's pain and suffering.

What you have is an anomaly. Clients expect their agencies to bow and scrape to their wishes, while at the same time ignoring agency needs for maintaining sanity, adhering to the schedule and producing the most carefully thought-out advertising.

This situation is often aggravated by the fact that client marketing people are sometimes not qualified to guide the agencies and are therefore bent on control rather than cooperation. Also, politics constantly threatens client relationships, with agencies attempting to invade the turf of other agencies in an effort to woo their clients and reap the bounty—a kind of internecine warfare.

Ron had retained consultant Dave Martin to guide management in dealing with these stresses and strains. To help Dave in seeking remedies, I sent him a memorandum in January of 1995 clarifying what I felt were the critical issues—many of which exist across the entire spectrum of advertising agencies:

1. No logic to the modus operandi. A helter-skelter approach to virtually everything we do.

2. No ability to hold to the mandates for a sane and workable process for turning out the advertising.

3. No understanding and sensitivity to the problems that cause a breakdown in quality control, which not only have a direct relationship to individual responsibility but also to timeframes and resources.

4. An acceptance of unreasonable timeframes as an appropriate way to operate on a permanent basis, simply because employees have repeatedly demonstrated the ability to turn out work under emergency conditions.

5. No attention to the morale implications of obligatory timeframes for the completion of projects that ignore practical realities.

6. No willingness to insist that clients understand they cannot have everything "immediately."

7. A fragmented Art Department with too many "chiefs" reporting to Ron, diminishing his ability to understand the problems requiring attention.

8. An absence of an adequate level of experienced sub leadership in the Account Management department, resulting in a weak marketing base to drive the creative process.

9. Inadequate copy department resources to serve the full range of clients and achieve the strongest, most impactful and highest quality copy platforms.

Ron gave lip service to these problems, but did little to accord them serious attention. Jim wrote them off as "just the way advertising is." Both allowed a sense of guilt to develop among those devoted employees who wanted to go home at the end of the 8:30 to 5:00 workday so they could have a life apart from the agency. Little by little, values so important to our culture were breaking down.

Exactly what were these values that were so critical to our culture? On December 17, 1998, I issued the following summary spelling out what I believed we were all about:

One of America's premier Direct Response advertising agencies.

Clients that read like a who's who of the corporate world.

An unequalled expertise in Direct Response telecom marketing.

A 15-year track record of success.

Uninterrupted growth year to year.

A dynamic, challenging environment.

A workplace filled with high spirits and enthusiasm.

An atmosphere that was fun and exciting.

Awards that represent the hallmarks of success.

A state-of-the-art facility, second to none.

Leadership in creative technology.

An increasing acumen in the interactive world.

The freedom to make a difference.

A culture based on friends and family.

Great creatives who are also skilled marketers.

The ability to "turn around on a dime."

A commitment to quality, integrity and creativity.

An owner who never stops giving "attaboys."

A Human Resources department that's really human.

A staff that loves to party.

An every day learning curve.

A dedication to promoting from within.

A big company that has never lost the small company touch.

The erosion of these values in the years ahead would take a heavy toll on the agency's culture, on our Direct Marketing leadership and on our bottom line.

One of the burdensome distractions for employees in an advertising agency culture is the balancing act of trying to get work done while being summoned to one meeting after another. There are creative brief meetings, creative review meetings, idea generation brainstorming, client creative presentations, client revision sessions, project status meetings, art department meetings, copy department meetings, marketing meetings, operations meetings, production meetings and finance meetings.

By far, the most important and necessary of these meetings is the Creative Brief. For the uninitiated, the anatomy of a Creative Brief offers a glimpse into how ad agency projects are put into motion after clients give marketing people their marching orders.

Different agencies do Creative Briefs in different ways. They are usually prepared and presented by Account Management (the marketers) in a forum that includes the creative, production and media staffers assigned to carry out the particular projects. The problem with these briefs is that they are sometimes lacking in the substance necessary for the creatives to go away and develop strong advertising. Marketers are known to abdicate this responsibility and put it on the heads of the creative specialists. Because of that, I was asked in December of 1998 to author a primer spelling out—for the benefit of the marketers—how to make sure their briefs covered all bases.

CHAPTER 3

WRITING A GREAT CREATIVE BRIEF

By Allen Stone
Vice President/Creative Director

Contents
Section One: An Introduction
Section Two: An Overview
Section Three: The Brief Itself
Section Four: The Support You Need

SECTION ONE

An Introduction

Writing a great Creative Brief calls, initially, for an understanding that the word "creative" may be misleading. Because, even though a brief deals with creative direction it is, in reality, a marketing function. So the first guideline to helping you write and deliver a great Creative Brief is to maintain a marketing mindset. Because impactful creative springs from a base of solid marketing. Anything less than that will compromise the strength of the creative work.

First, consider what not to do.

* Do not leave all the decisions and thinking to the copywriters and artists. Keep in mind that, though they may have abundant marketing savvy, they are executors and not marketers.

* Do not expect solutions to complex client-related marketing problems to materialize out of thin air. They need to be carefully thought out and presented as part of the Creative Brief.

* Do not use words like "breakthrough creative" without providing a Creative Brief that gives the artists and designers everything they need to know to accomplish that.

* Do not hesitate to offer strong and precise creative direction but leave basic idea generation to the creative people.

* Do not fail to prioritize the flow of product benefits so Creatives understand where to start, where to go and where to end, thus avoiding redirects, either by agency marketers or clients.

* Do not fail to work hard at finding the right selling propositions and the best words in the Creative Brief to express them in the least ambiguous and most exciting way.

The need to work hard and think deeply flows through every section of this document. An effective Creative Brief cannot be produced "on the run." All materials in the brief should be of substance, based on the results desired and sufficient to gain acceptance from everyone attending the brief. Also, when possible, there should be client approval of the brief before it is presented in the agency. Otherwise your brief could end up invalid in the eyes of the client, and that could mean going back to the drawing board.

Keep in mind that when you have written your Creative Brief, you are only halfway there. Without effective communication at the brief presentation, comprehension will be lacking.

Next, an examination of why a good Creative Brief requires exhaustive research and analysis.

SECTION TWO

An Overview

Your brief must be clear and concise, with a logic that links it throughout. It should offer insights into the mindset of the target audience . . . including specifics that define the given businesses or consumers who will receive the direct response advertising: size and type of business, competitive advantages and disadvantages, ethnic considerations, motivational factors, computer literacy, age bracket, education level, economic strata, negative and positive attitudes and proclivities. Whatever information helps the creatives see their mission through the eyes of the target audiences must be outlined in the Creative Brief.

Briefs must take into consideration that the marketplace is ever-changing . . . that an agency's mission is not only to build strong selling vehicles firmly based on strategic planning and quality execution, but also to guide our clients through the constantly changing marketplace environment. Briefs must recognize that messages inspiring product purchases five years ago may be totally ineffective today.

Summing up, the Creative Brief—in simple English—must provide single minded direction to the copywriters and designers, a well-defined statement of client goals and objectives plus a clear understanding of budgetary and production considerations.

Scanning the requirements set forth on the Creative Brief form might lead to the conclusion that the form is reasonably simple and straightforward. But "form" is one thing, "substance" is another and that's where we go from here.

SECTION THREE

The Brief Itself

The Creative Brief form must be precise and logical in listing and defining the individual requirements. It must be easy to understand the top-to-bottom categories. But, its excellence depends on "putting meat on the bones." That's where simplicity ends and meaningful marketing begins . . . the kind of insightful marketing that inspires the most convincing creative solutions.

There will be sections of the form that do not require elaboration. In other areas, your brief will need to present carefully worked-out guidelines on specific subjects common to every assignment. To wit:

1. Client objectives for the job.

State exactly what you are trying to achieve for the client. Be explicit. Forget "round" phrases. Lay down facts and figures. Is the primary goal branding, direct sales, repeat purchases, image perception, churn reduction, etc? What is the desired response? What does the client see as impediments to achieving its objectives? What are the client mandates the agency must address in completing the work?

2. The key brand positioning.

This is, indeed, a "key" to the entire communications process. The brief must spell out everything we know about the brand, the market for the brand, what makes it different from other brands and what motivates purchase. Before you write the brand positioning into the brief, check to make sure that one does not already exist. It may be that the client's general agency has a positioning applicable to the direct marketing. Consumers and businesses look at brands in several ways.

*   Is Brand X cheaper than Brand Y?

*   Will the brand you're promoting be perceived as better than similar brands?

* Does the brand fit the specific needs of the prospects you're targeting?

* What is the strongest sales motivating attribute?

The brand positioning is a major factor in strengthening the overall creative strategy. And of all the requirements you list on your form, the one that follows is central to the pursuit of creative solutions.

3. Know who you're talking to.

The creative team must know exactly who their work is aimed at. Be precise in defining the nature of your target audience—business or consumer. Cover the demographic, behavioral and attitudinal elements discussed in the Overview section of this document.

4. How the product is perceived.

Here you expand on the brand positioning. Do your research. Find out if the prospects you are aiming at with the advertising already have perceptions about the product or service . . . its features and benefits. If not, describe on your brief form how you want the prospects to think, feel and react as a result of your communication to them.

5. The single, most important purchase proposition.

This is critical to the creative development . . . an open door to the BIG IDEA. It must be a single-minded proposition, the most differentiating message you can give the target audience up front in the piece of advertising. Finding this big idea means that you should review the rest of your brief and the product information provided by the client, think about every product or service benefit and decide which one will represent the strongest, most persuasive proposition.

6. The focus on credibility.

What good is your single, most important purchase proposition if it is not believed? So it will need substantiation in your Creative Brief. Make sure your product or service attributes are clearly and convincingly outlined in your brief. Suggest the use of customer testimonials if appropriate and available.

Finally, let's not forget the support material you should be sure to include as a component of your Creative Brief. That's our wrap up section.

SECTION FOUR

The Support You Need

This information will not only help you write a great Creative Brief, it will contribute to the ability of the copywriters and designers to produce better work.

* Provide whatever useful information you can get . . . from the client or from your own research.

* Get hold of competitive promotions, together with results if possible.

* Obtain whatever work has previously been completed for the account, by other general or direct agencies, on television and in print ads.

* If the product or service is also handled by sales people or through telemarketing, acquaint yourself with their pitches and techniques.

* If possible, allow the creative people to try the product or service they are being asked to promote.

Closing statement

This document contains some, but by no means all, of the pointers that will enhance your ability to write and deliver a great Creative Brief. Even though the Creative Brief form will be used in the agency on a consistent basis by each business unit, you should not feel slavishly bound or straight-jacketed in pursuing your own pathways aimed at producing the strongest possible brief. Know your client. Know what your client expects. And use your own ingenuity in developing the information and strategies that will make your Creative Brief a standout.

I'd like to say that my Creative Brief document opened a new era of marketing professionalism in the agency. But unfortunately it didn't, because this exposition never saw the light of day.

That is not to say that all of our marketers were weak in writing and presenting Creative Briefs. Several were quite good at it. Unfortunately, the marketing supervisors seldom reviewed the Creative Briefs completed by their direct reports, seldom mentored those who needed guidance, and almost never submitted briefs to clients for approval prior to presentation in the agency. When this is the case, it can lead to problems later in the process with supervisors changing directions and blaming the Creatives for losing focus, when the real culprit is insufficient marketing direction.

The avalanche of meetings in ad agencies, including sometimes two to four Creative Briefs a day, is one reason why agency staffers must put in time after hours to get work done. The industry needs to collect itself up and do something to ameliorate this problem. It is a catalyst to burnout and damaging to the creative environment.

Did management at Devon Direct escape this meeting binge? Not on your life! And that's a comic opera in itself.

CHAPTER 4

THE MANAGEMENT MEETINGS

I once had a college professor who was fond of using the expression verbal slobber when referring to excess verbiage. I know of no better way to describe the half-day management meetings I was obliged to attend every Wednesday, presided over by Ron Greene and consultant Dave Martin. Despite good intentions, these meetings were not very inspirational. They were little more than exercises in futility, droning on with lots of excess verbiage but little substance. It was difficult to keep from closing your eyes or your mind. Each week, the list of subjects to be taken up in the interest of improving operations was distributed in advance. If you were there observing these meetings, here's what you might expect in the way of agendas:

On one Wednesday, it was . . .

* A fresh look at organizational needs as changes and turnover occur.

* The issue of promotions and position levels within the agency.

* A strong need to discuss the philosophy underlying the global issues.

* Various ideas and initiatives to address recruiting needs.

* What does the agency want to be?

* What is the role of the management committee?

Another Wednesday we covered . . .

* Hiring qualified people because of the effect on new business growth.

* Attract one new client with $2-5MM revenue potential.

* Each department head to behave maturely and professionally.

* How to attract and retain supervisor/director level employees.

And there was the Wednesday we considered these issues . . .

* Be more honest. Avoid politics.

* Eliminate the suspicion of hidden agendas.

* More open discussions. Faster resolution of issues.

* More openness rather than competing for Ron's attention.

All legitimate subjects to be sure. Ron and Dave were right to put them on the table. In response, each manager tried to make an impressive statement, to which others would invariably take issue. Most of the managers were intent on posturing rather than problem solving. Within the group there were a couple of managers I respected and they were as frustrated as I was with having to waste time on these unproductive talkfests. To everyone's relief, the management meetings were eventually cut back to once a month. The only thing I missed was the muffins and bagels that greeted us at the start of each weekly meeting.

About Dave Martin. Very sincere. Very dedicated. Very ebullient. And very costly. But not very steeped in the whys and wherefores of the advertising profession and given to invoking textbook applications not germane to workplace realities. In truth, he should have paid us for the learning process.

Everybody liked Dave but questioned his value to the agency. He arrived for management meetings with his briefcase bulging, offered observations and made pronouncements relating to the talk around the table, but I honestly do not recall any insights that could be characterized as profound and pithy. I will admit that we enjoyed having Dave in our midst, even as we had to tolerate the endless yarns about his days with the military. He had an appealing sense of humor and a genuine concern for the agency. My principle reservation was that the money Ron paid him through all those years probably could have funded a barrel full of merit increases and bonuses.

As if all the meetings were not enough, Ron Greene had a penchant for landing down on the employees with time-consuming extra-curricular projects that had little to do with client activity and lent to the pressure keg. There were learning curves on every conceivable aspect of the agency's operations—laboriously prepared and presented in the boardroom to the entire staff. They were crammed with information, artfully conceived and carried out. But they robbed too much time from the real work.

I staged one of these learning curves along with several of my copy department colleagues. We called it "Making Words Work." As part of the presentation, I identified four basic types of copywriting mentalities, four distinct kinds of advertising writers—each with advantages and disadvantages. This will give you some idea of how copywriters pursue the craft of using the written word effectively.

1. **The Creative Flash:** The writer who explodes with brilliant bursts of genius. This writer bristles with magical phrases. He or she is innovative, poetic, sparkling and capable of inventing new ways of saying old things. It is this writer about whom every other writer says: "I wish I'd thought of that." The problem is those who read this writer's copy admire its beauty but often don't buy the product.

2. **The Craftsman:** Here's the writer so thoroughly experienced that he or she goes by rote—turning out one project after another by simply doing what he or she has always done. This writer's value is in completing twice as many programs as anyone else in half the time. But sometimes the work, although professionally up to standard, can be a bit tired, repetitious and lacking in inventiveness since it falls into the trap of relying on past accomplishments as the sole barometer for future success.

3. **The Bricklayer:** This is the writer who puts words into place one by one, ever so carefully. Just like a journeyman bricklayer. The words are assembled and reassembled until the paragraph is flawless in structure and grammar. Every paragraph is regarded as a unit to be painstakingly built, honed and refined. This writer can fall victim to not being able to stop changing the structure until, at last, he or she loses perspective.

4. **The Disciplined Thinker:** Here you have the writer who sets up priorities, makes certain the copy covers every necessary element, meticulously outlines and reinforces every point that could contribute to the success of the program. But copy from this writer can become too burdensome, too much for the reader and potential customer to plow through.

I'm sure you've drawn the obvious conclusion. The ideal writer is one who is able to operate with all four mindsets—perhaps a bit more proficient at one or the other. Advertising writers do not have to be great at everything but should be great at something and able to borrow the best from their colleagues.

They do have to know how design and copy work together . . . how to write with the brain and not the hand . . . where to start, where to go and where to finish . . . that the strategy gives birth to the words . . . how to be innovative and clever, but credible . . . how to keep an open mind to a better way . . . especially how to be convincing about product benefits and drive prospects to the point of decision.

They also need to tolerate the agency/client tug-o-war on the question of copy length. There are clients who are minimalists. They want minimal copy in their advertising, reasoning that the public does not like to read. Other clients are maximalists. They want to throw the kitchen sink into the copy.

Here's the dilemma. Minimalist clients are given to coming back with additional information they want included, ending up with as many words as those clients who prefer long copy, who then want it shorter.

It's another challenge to sanity.

So much for the learning curves. I also found myself borrowing time to create what I was told should be visually interesting motivational posters mirroring entrepreneurial attributes that built the agency and aimed at firing up the staff, such as:

The Fine Points Of . . .

ENERGETIC LEADERSHIP

* Accountability

* Productivity

* Dependability

* Communication

* Inspiration

* Motivation

* Organizational skills

* Logistical skills

* People skills

At Euro RSCG Devon Direct, everyone is a leader in meeting the exciting challenge of taking our agency forward and enjoying the rewards that come with success.

GRAB THE BRASS RING! TAKE UP THE GAUNTLET! MAKE THINGS HAPPEN!

Other culture values developed into posters were:

1. Goal-oriented

2. Results-oriented

3. Vision-guided

4. Innovative

5. Creative

6. Lean/profit motivated

7. Hunger for growth and achievement

8. Hands-on

9. Flexibility

10. Action-oriented

11. Personal pride

Once a week, for 12 weeks, a full-size poster was positioned in the agency's lobby and miniature versions were displayed at various locations throughout the company. The problem was, few employees needed to be fired up or reenergized. They were already working at a feverish pace and giving their all. But, I must say, the posters were beautifully done and well received.

Topping it off, department heads were instructed to establish committees that were tasked with producing in-depth examinations of subjects Ron felt needed attention and action . . . areas where employees were perceived to be delinquent.

The committee under my leadership was the only one that made a significant contribution. Others quietly withdrew and hoped they wouldn't be called on the carpet. Given the press of daily priorities, they invariably escaped notice—as was often the case in the agency with best-laid plans and good intentions.

My committee's subject was *Communication and Teamwork*. It was felt that serious problems in the agency derived from the absence of effective communication and teamwork. We spent many weeks studying these problems and determining solutions, then assembling and publishing a landmark document—praised not only by Ron Greene but by the entire management and all agency departments.

Our purpose in this policy statement was to help achieve maximum individual accountability and operating efficiency, to promote morale and enhance job satisfaction—through improved communication agency-wide as well as at all inter—and intra-departmental levels. We defined the principles of this effort as:

Accept the need for *interdependence*.

Create and maintain *respectful relationships*.

Hold one another *accountable* for information.

Keep an *open mind* to ensure positive results.

Commit the *time and energy* needed for exceptional thinking.

Always *follow up* promptly.

Always *listen* actively.

Consider *what's best* for the agency.

Be *concise, constructive* and *issue-oriented.*

Always confirm your understanding.

Support decisions by those authorized to make them.

As to our goals and objectives, implementation of these initiatives was deemed as essential so that:

* All employees understand how all departments work together to ensure the viability of the process.

* Each employee knows what is expected of him or her.

* Resolution of issues is quickly expedited.

* A shared vision promotes understanding and cooperation.

* The delegation of tasks produces the desired result.

* Each employee will feel they are appreciated as an individual.

* Supervisors at all levels are aware of the status of each project and any problems.

* Teams working on different avenues of activity for the same client understand the total picture and plan and prioritize to ensure the availability of resources and acceptability of timeframes.

* Employees are never in the dark on critical issues and comprehend the totality of commitments.

* Timely, objective feedback is assured at all levels.

* Projects can be reviewed at appropriate times, including weekly status meetings.

* Daily requirements subject to revision can be effectively addressed and met.

* The agency can ensure fidelity to budgets.

* The ability to respond to client expectations can be enhanced.

* Clients can fully appreciate what it takes to produce highest quality and highest impact work.

* Clients can understand their own obligations as part of the partnership.

* A fully productive relationship can be maintained with every client.

These purposes, principles, goals and objectives plus the excerpted passages in the next chapter, taken from the actual policy statement (space precludes presentation of the entire statement)—demonstrate the problem/solution magnitude of communication and teamwork in an advertising agency setting. The precepts covered in the document can be broadly applied down the line in the business world. Especially since advertising agencies are not the only companies that give scant attention to effective communication and teamwork.

Who among us has not suffered the frustration of going through the gyrations of making contact with a company without being put in touch with a real person who can effectively communicate and solve a problem? I dare say, we are all fed up with press 1, press 2, etc.

Just recently, I went through a press this and press that in an effort to reach a company I wanted to do business with. I got one of those "all our reps are busy" messages and was shifted to their voicemail with a promise to call me back. I'm still waiting. That same day, I tried to schedule an appointment with my physician. Three times, I called. Three times, I was told to hold. Three times, they never came back to the phone. Then there was the day I received a bill from a company involving a product I already paid for. I brought it to the company's attention and ignored the bill when they ignored me.

Which takes us to my committee's assault on the lost art of communication—applicable to an advertising agency, but with much to chew on for any business or industry. As you work your way through the following chapter, keep in mind that the efficacy of communication, when written, relies not only on matters of substance but also on the easy and fluent use of language . . . and when oral, the key operative words are diction, enunciation, intonation and articulation. Lessons I learned during 35 years as a broadcast journalist.

CHAPTER 5

COMMUNICATION AND TEAMWORK

The Team Ethic

The premise that flows through this entire document is the conclusion that a team ethic is central to any company's interactive process. No department or individual can be exempt from this understanding. The process cannot work in the absence of effective teamwork.

All employees must think of themselves as members of a team. Each must regard himself or herself as an integral part of the whole. Each must recognize the value of the others' efforts. No individual—whether supervisor or direct report—can be an outsider to the team ethic. Team members must cultivate trust in each other . . . share in the wins and losses . . . and be active participants in the decision-making process. This is critical to improved communication company-wide, within and between departments.

Team members working on a client project together, under the direction of a supervisor, should be empowered to move forward with project development. They should review the Creative Brief in advance of the brief itself and the start of any work. Once this is accomplished, the core team should pursue creative development unencumbered by repeated changes to the original creative direction. Recognizing at the same time that there is a "captain" of every effort, personally accountable for the end result . . . whose decisions must be respected and implemented.

Supervisors are charged with the responsibility to communicate the importance of the team ethic to their direct reports. These individuals should emphasize that the company's culture relies heavily on this team spirit in all areas of activity.

Effective application of the team ethic to resolve problems, exercise leadership, build relationships, promote morale, ease frustrations, manage schedules and maintain quality will be included as a measure of job performance.

Supervisors should make sure that the responsibilities of their direct reports as they apply to the company's process, are clear and that employees have an understanding of the impact of performing the duties that apply to their position. It is also important to the objective of promoting the team ethic that employees appreciate the functions of their counterparts in areas that also contribute to the process. Informational sessions should be conducted as appropriate to this understanding.

Cultivating and encouraging a positive, proactive team-like atmosphere through implementation of the practices and procedures outlined in this document is company policy.

Office Protocol

This section of the document deals with how to conduct day-to-day business when an employee wishes to enter or are in a colleague's office. And the appropriate way to carry on business when an employee is in his or her own office and meeting with a colleague or approached by a colleague.

At all times, an employee should ask permission to interrupt activity and confirm it is a good time to discuss a particular topic. If not, to schedule a time that is convenient for both parties.

When holding a meeting, let phone calls go into voicemail, unless an important call is expected. And keep in mind that face-to-face discussions with colleagues are preferable to going back and forth on email.

When leaving items for a person at their desk, leave a note and/or follow up voicemail or email to alert the recipient that this new item has been placed in their office and, if necessary, what action needs to be taken.

Meeting Process and Protocol

As someone once said:

"A model meeting is participated in by everybody monopolized by nobody, where everybody is somebody."

Determine if a formal meeting is necessary, or whether you can accomplish your goal via a more informal session or communication medium.

Ensure you will have all the information you need to conduct a satisfactory meeting.

Prepare the goal for the meeting.

Determine who should attend.

Decide when and where the meeting should be held.

Prepare a concise, logical agenda. Allot time to each agenda item, including time to recap before the meeting ends.

Reserve the meeting room and invite participants, giving as much notice as possible.

Give instructions on what participants should do to prepare for the meeting.

When calling a meeting with short notice, send an email or voicemail first.

Prepare for the meeting including preparation of meeting materials and, where time allows, distribute in advance.

Materials should be of substance based on results desired.

The meeting leader should review their role in advance.

Participants should ask for clarification of any agenda item prior to the meeting and come prepared to contribute.

If a participant expects to be late for a meeting—or absent from it—due to a last-minute urgent conflict, they should advise the meeting leader, as opposed to just showing up late or not at all.

Participants who are unable to attend should contact the meeting leader for pertinent information.

Those invited to attend should not bring additional people to a meeting unless discussed with and agreed to by the meeting leader.

Start the meeting on time. If participants know that you will not wait for them, they will learn to be prompt.

If a meeting runs longer than an hour, invite participants to take a break or get up and move around.

At the outset, discuss the purpose of the meeting, review the game plan and, at the end, get a consensus that the meeting goal was understood.

Begin with good news and end with good news.

If applicable, post your issue statement or meeting goal on the wall.

The meeting leader may ask someone to record ideas on a flip chart.

Keep the agenda on track. Any "off-the-topic" input can be deferred until another time.

Participants should write down questions to be asked when called for.

Any differing views should be reconciled.

The meeting leader should discourage any non-productive input.

At the end of the meeting, determine next steps, due dates and who's responsible for what.

Get acceptance and commitments from everyone.

Participants should follow through as required.

—in the words of the inimitable Oscar Wilde

"In a study of one class of graduates of a prestigious business school, professors predicted the future success of each graduate, using such factors as entrepreneurship, assertiveness, boldness, creativity and so forth. After 10 years, these graduates were revisited. For those who had achieved top management positions, none of the established criteria held up. The only common factors were a sense of humor and the ability to run a great meeting."

Communications Channels

1. One-on-one, in-person meetings continue to be an essential channel of communication. Appropriate usage would include:

    *   When time is of the essence, especially when decisions are needed to move forward.

    *   When the nature of the subject requires face-to-face explanation and discussion.

* To resolve conflicts or open issues.

* To discuss delicate issues involving employee performance.

* When personal or confidential issues require it.

* When you need confirmation that a given action has been taken.

2. Guidelines for telephone courtesy and voicemail.

   * Identify yourself when receiving or placing a call.

   * When placing a call, explain your purpose and ask if it's a convenient time to talk.

   * If your call goes into voicemail, leave a brief message and be sure to include your name, extension number and the time of your call.

   * Keep in mind that effective communication depends on frequent checking of voicemail.

   * Be sure to update your voicemail greeting whenever you plan to be out of the office for a day or more.

   * Do not depend solely on voicemail in situations of utmost urgency.

3. The appropriate use of email.

   * It should be a topic for discussion between managers and direct reports to ensure effective use and prevent abuse.

   * It should always be used in the best interests of the company.

   * It should be checked on a regular basis throughout the day.

   * Other than matters involving confidentiality, anyone mentioned in an email should be copied.

* Email should be used when personal consultation is not required, when there is the need to schedule a meeting, when requesting or providing tangible information, as an efficient way to pass along ideas, and to follow up and confirm conversations and conference calls.

4. The inappropriate use of email.

* In the place of any meeting that requires substantive participation.

* To resolve conflicts or open issues. In this case, parties should get together in-person.

* To advise another employee that their responsibilities in regard to a specific project have not been met. This requires face-to-face discussion.

Inter-Departmental Communication

It begins with the understanding that no department is an island unto itself. Respect for each department's priorities, contributions and challenges—combined with an appreciation of inter-departmental dependency—will promote teamwork and enhance morale.

Moreover, inter-departmental communication recognizes that a disciplined interactive process is key to a company's ability to maintain a competitive edge through maximum efficiency and cost-effectiveness, as well as the highest possible product quality.

To this end, communication and follow-up must occur in a timely fashion to ensure:

Productive planning, preparation and organization.

Examples: Meetings and presentations.

Appropriate use and management of resources.

Examples: Understanding/communicating the magnitude of assignments.

Agreement on timeframes prior to commitments.

Examples: Client-related and company-related projects.

The avoidance of breakdowns as a job progresses.

Examples: Managing changes, making revisions and coping with redirects.

The avoidance of wasted time.

Examples: Excessive corridor conversation. Leaving information on an individual's desk.

Adherence to administrative responsibilities

Examples: Timesheets, expense reports, performance appraisals.

In addition, top management has a responsibility to facilitate a continuing flow of information throughout the company.

Intra-Departmental Communication

To enhance the company's inter-departmental communication, effective interaction is essential within departments—so all who participate in the company's process are on the same track.

* Supervisor-subordinate communication. Supervisors should regularly communicate with their team to ensure that:

> Vital news and information are relayed in a timely manner.

> Direct reports are effectively communicating with their direct reports.

> Important email announcements are discussed before and/or after they have been distributed.

> Subordinates understand the level of routine communication required by their supervisors.

Additionally, once a decision or course of action has been agreed upon, supervisors should limit their involvement to an advisory role. This will empower their teams to follow through uninhibited.

* Subordinate-supervisor communication. Subordinates should communicate frequently with their supervisors to make sure that:

    > Relevant issues are addressed in a timely manner.

    > Supervisors are not "blindsided" by recurring problems.

* Communication between colleagues. Members of teams are encouraged to communicate with one another to make certain that:

    > Resources are being used efficiently.

    > Ideas and information are being shared.

    > Effective planning is taking place.

    > No one is left out of the loop on project status.

Additionally, to facilitate the cross-pollination of ideas, employees are encouraged to seek project-related feedback from their colleagues, as needed.

* Confidential information. The two basic essentials:

    > Employees who pass along confidential information to anyone who needs to know should clearly communicate the confidential nature of the matter.

    > Employees who receive confidential information are responsible for keeping that information confidential. This includes awareness that others may overhear conversations in cubicles or corridors.

* Scheduled absences. To ensure that work does not slip through the cracks, due to time spent away from the office, employees should make fellow department members aware of the following points as far in advance as possible:

    > Project status.

    > Key contact people from other departments.

    > Who is to "cover" for the absent employee.

Interaction With Clients

Effective communication is an important adjunct to successful agency/ client interaction.

* Its aim must be meeting the client's goals and objectives and creating a true partnership, while furthering the company's ability to safeguard its own process when threatened by client demands.

* It must be organized and focused to be effective.

* It benefits from company personnel being problem solvers and decision-makers.

* It facilitates the agency's creative, approval and control processes.

* It aids in the successful negotiation of client-mandated schedules and empowers the agency's Account Management Department to be proactive rather than reactive.

* It means emphasizing the agency's recommendations when presenting clients with multiple choices in advertising creative.

* It should not ignore the value of social interaction.

* It is enhanced when new members of an agency team serving a client are schooled in the essential elements of communication pertaining to that client.

Account Management members should communicate with clients to make sure they understand that the agency's creative process depends on receiving complete and accurate information from the client in a timely manner. Otherwise, timeframes can be jeopardized. With this in mind, Account teams are encouraged to educate clients about topics like:

* The creative process for development of the advertising.

* The up-front and ongoing information needed for guiding agency personnel assigned to develop the advertising.

* How cost and scheduling are affected by last minute, client-ordered changes to the advertising.

* The need for adherence to contractual and financial obligations.

Account Management teams should encourage clients to assist the agency in understanding their internal processes. Considerations such as:

* The nature and extent of information they customarily provide when assigning work to an agency.

* Their required approval of the advertising and sending it into the marketplace.

* Available client educational forums to enhance the agency's knowledge of product, branding, competitive environment, etc.

* Client goals, objectives and priorities.

Client visits to the agency provide a valuable opportunity to promote effective communication by presenting the agency in a friendly, positive light. To this end, employees are encouraged to:

* Post email messages announcing client visits.

* Post welcome signs in the lobby on the day of a client visit.

*   Make clients feel welcome when encountered in hallways, lunchrooms, etc.

*   Make sure workstations are neat and clean.

*   Make sure workstations are occupied so employees can communicate the unique functions of their department to clients touring the agency.

In presenting this treatise on effective communication and teamwork, my hope is that professionals who read it—whether or not in advertising—might ponder what I have written in the interest of finding useful catalysts to influencing and refining the interactive processes in their own companies.

Attention to these matters is critical to a company's ability to operate efficiently, to an employee's capacity to function productively and to establishing harmonious relationships with customers and clients.

CHAPTER 6

THE STAFF ENDURED

The burgeoning problems at Devon Direct notwithstanding, the staff remained convinced they were in the right place. They were especially thankful for the business-building acumen of the agency's savior . . . that powerhouse of Southern charm and marketing savvy, Ed Carter. A bulldozing, foot stomping, chain smoking telecom pioneer, Ed brought us virtually every big name, big budget client that fueled our growth and kept us afloat. He took us into Sprint, MCI, Bell Atlantic, British Telecom and Cellnet. Carter was the proverbial "bull-in-the-china-shop" who beat up on clients and their employees, cursing them out when they refused to recognize the brilliance of his ideas, invariably wearing out his welcome with every client. Even Greene and Perry as well as the entire staff felt the sting of his presence but never questioned his value to the agency.

When Ed Carter was no longer a part of our scene, it was a wound that would never heal and a harbinger of the downturn ahead. We were never able to find anyone equal to Carter in acquiring new business for the agency.

Before long, Jim Perry lost his tolerance for the business and determined to spend his days sailing the Caribbean with Marianne Croze. An agency principle with undeniable marketing skills, she bowed out of her position as a vice president following years of accomplishing her goals through use of punishing tactics on the creative staff. Like Murphy Brown, she went through secretaries and the marketers she supervised at lightning speed. Oh but did she ever know how to turn on the charm when working with the clients!

I had the impression that the parting of Ron and Jim was not amicable. None-the-less, I was saddened to see Jim depart, since I was one of the few people in the agency he truly admired. With Jim, there was no bull. He always told it like it was whereas Ron preferred to tell it like he wanted it to be.

We persisted in efforts to attract new clients, while losing our ability to turn them into long-term relationships. We established annual planning meetings to lay out priorities that were hardly ever met. Ron held summertime management problem-solving sessions at his Long Beach Island home on the Jersey shore. Few problems were solved. Even so, to his credit, Ron continued to fatten paychecks, hand out bonuses and treat the staff to lavish holiday parties. In addition to our Berwyn, Pennsylvania headquarters, we had opened an office in New York, another in London, one in California and, viewing the Web as the ultimate direct marketing channel, we had established a firm grip on Internet advertising. Then we did something that was totally out of character and would seal our fate.

Instead of maintaining the Ed Carter focus on acquiring clients that represented established brands the public recognized and respected, we changed course, locking ourselves into a pursuit of the Dot Coms as well as other types of technology companies.

We were led down this ill-conceived path by Bob Vogel, hired to head up business development because of his grip on advertising technology and direct marketing experience. He was undeniably smart. Especially in his ability to convince Ron Greene that he was a valuable asset to the company. His memos in this regard were brilliantly orchestrated.

Agency staffers were turned off by his cavalier treatment and arbitrary manner. Ron asked me to talk with him about that, which I did—to no avail. Worst of all, he had a one track mind on what kind of clients were best for Devon Direct. Time and again in management sessions, I asked why we were putting so many eggs in the Dot Com and technology basket. Invariably, Vogel would reply: "Allen, that's where the potential is." To which I would always respond: "Bob, don't talk to me about potential, talk to me about security."

It was five years before Ron woke up to the fact that this pursuit of potential was not working. Nor was any other business acquisition plan taking us where we needed to be. Many of the Dot Coms had died. We got in with companies like Enron and SunMicrosystems. They went out faster than they came in. It came to pass that Bob Vogel was out too.

Fortunately for Ron, he had already sold the company. The employees speculated that he had seen the handwriting on the wall, that he knew Devon couldn't stay the course without Ed Carter, and that's why he decided to sell. When he announced that decision to the company, he tried to put a good face on it—predicting that our Euro RSCG connection would help drive the agency's growth to new plateaus of success.

It was not to be. Euro was no sugar daddy. And Devon would soon become the poor relative, increasingly unable to post the annual Euro mandated profit margins. It was inevitable that we were heading for hard times. And Ron Greene, under the thumb of Bob Schmetterer— Havas holding company president-COO and chairman-CEO of Euro RSCG—instead of acting to strengthen his own leadership, fell into a pattern of reaction and inaction. Inevitably, the employees were drained of their confidence in his ability to lead.

CHAPTER 7

BOB SCHMETTERER
THE B.M.O.C OF ADVERTISING

Before his hasty departure in January, 2004 following rumors of a power struggle within Havas, Schmetterer was indeed, to revive an old expression, the Big Man on Campus. And in many respects, deservedly. An industry innovator, Schmetterer commanded attention for his charm, wit and style but mostly his intellect and out-of-the box thinking. An advertising icon, weary with traditional marketing and passionate in his devotion to business strategies based on big creative ideas—Bob Schmetterer was bigger-than-life in his leadership of the Euro RSCG Worldwide network. He was constantly in demand to keynote major advertising events. Read his book *LEAP* and you'll understand why his prominence came from more than his charisma.

Schmetterer's global focus for all Euro RSCG clients was the development of CBIs—Creative Business Ideas which, in his book, he describes as "ideas that not only sell products and establish brands, but, more important, transform entire companies and categories." Ideas unparalleled in their power that "take a company's business strategies light-years beyond its CEO's dreams." A tall order? Schmetterer did not disagree.

Too tall, it turned out, for Euro RSCG Devon Direct. We labored to incorporate Schmetterer's imperative into our mindset and make it our unwavering commitment. But it didn't happen. The closest we came to it was in work we did for GMAC and Weekly Reader. As good as this work was and as much as it broke new ground for these clients, it was still not in the league of Creative Business Ideas as defined by Schmetterer. Creativity had always been at the heart of our advertising strategy. We were excellent at crafting messages of meaning and value for our clients. We knew how to adapt to and capitalize on marketplaces undergoing rapid evolution. Our flawless creative executions produced meaningful results for our clients. So why was it that we could not seem to meet Schmetterer's mandate for breakthrough solutions that go beyond traditional advertising, and that ultimately transform the nature of business itself? That was the question a frustrated Ron Greene put to me.

I confess to being surprised that he didn't know the answer to that himself.

I told Ron our people would love to come up with brilliant Creative Business Ideas. But to begin with, we were not working in the expansive medium of television, which affords greater opportunity for grandiose thinking and the budgets for implementation of big ideas. We were a nuts and bolts Direct Marketing agency, grinding out advertising like hamburger, taking orders from clients and delivering the goods on budget and under timeframes that did not allow for the thinking and strategizing required to develop Creative Business Ideas. So how to do it? I proposed the formation of an agency-wide think tank that would take up the CBI problem on a regular schedule and include Euro involvement as well as client input.

As to client participation in the development of CBIs, Schmetterer's thoughts on the importance of that are worth quoting from his book.

"High-level corporate acceptance of creative thinking is a prerequisite for Creative Business Ideas. Without it, a CBI cannot survive. It's that simple." Schmetterer goes on to explain that creativity must start at the top, that client CEOs must become the champions of great

ideas . . . that CBIs must be the culmination of client and agency
strategists spending countless hours together in a warroom.

So that doomed our ability to orchestrate CBIs right from the start. No
agency-wide CBI think tank was ever established at Devon. There was no
input from Euro. And no attempt was ever made to bring clients into a
meaningful partnership for the development of big ideas. Which brings
us to a further examination of this Creative Business Ideas notion.

In his book, Bob Schmetterer talks of the proven power of CBIs. He
says they've worked wonders. For example in capitalizing on safety in
branding Volvo automobiles. In convincing Americans to choose
Perdue chickens as a commodity bought not just by the pound, but by
the brand. And in changing the way people consume music with the
Sony Walkman, an industry first that transformed the marketplace by
putting together headphones and a portable tape player.

Perhaps the most intriguing CBI was the decision by a small Euro agency
in Buenos Aires, Argentina which—instead of executing an ad
campaign to sell a riverfront real estate development—advised the
client to build an instant landmark. A pedestrian footbridge that would
attract tourists and residents to the riverfront, and to the real estate
development. An Insightful and ingenious CBI, according to Bob
Schmetterer.

Schmetterer says it must be understood that Creative Business Ideas
mean the end of advertising as it has been traditionally defined and
the "beginning of something new." The world has changed, says
Schmetterer, and agencies have to play by new rules.

One of these new rules, according to Schmetterer, would require
agencies to literally break down walls. No more individual offices,
instead a melting pot of employees from all departments in one big
bullpen . . . interacting with each other in an effort to crash through
the barriers and ring the curtain up on brilliant Creative Business
Ideas. Maybe that would work in some agency environments, but my
own view is that the more peace and quiet you provide, the more you
get back in strategic thinking and quality work.

I cannot deny that Schmetterer made a strong case for this revolutionary approach that would, in his view, "instill the magic of creativity into the very fabric and nature of business itself." Indeed, it is hard to argue against Schmetterer's genius in giving birth to this novel idea. But are other bigtime agencies outside of Euro RSCG jumping onto the Schmetterer bandwagon? I don't see that happening. Most ad agencies, whether Direct Response or general advertising, are doing as they've always done and not embracing Schmetterer's CBI strategy as the ultimate channel for winning new clients and scoring successes in the marketplace.

Good advertising agencies fully understand the need to develop impactful creative ideas that are sensitive to real world business and consumer needs. Schmetterer simply put another label and another spin on strategic advertising methodology. His CBI proposition was grandly conceived but it did not change a thing in the lexicon of agency practices for serving clients and achieving victories in the marketplace. Agencies constantly strive to craft bold new creative platforms that put their clients ahead of the competition. They know that, given today's marketplace sensibilities, the requirement for new thinking and bigger ideas is urgent. No question that Bob Schmetterer is an intellectual of boundless capacity with a proven track record. But he is not the only innovator in the advertising business. His tactical mistake, in my view, was allowing himself to become an out-of-touch visionary, operating from the summit of his own Mount Olympus. And though he saw CBIs as the pathway to a creative revolution, agencies will invent and reinvent their own pathways, as they have always done. What's more, Schmetterer's sudden retirement in the midst of declining revenues at Euro RSCG did not speak well for the power of Creative Business Ideas.

Before he departed, Euro did make what turned out to be a feeble attempt to test a plan for implementing Schmetterer's philosophy and getting its agencies involved with each other.

This plan was called The Power Of One. It aligned Devon Direct with eight other North American sister agencies to break down barriers, give clients more bang for the buck, provide innovative new ways to efficiently deliver integrated marketing solutions and a potent edge in crafting powerful creative strategies. Good logic. But it proved to be nothing beyond high-sounding words. Perhaps understandably, in that some of our sister agencies saw no benefit in getting us involved with their clients. Those that did often threw up roadblocks that made integration of our efforts a lost cause. Cooperation invariably gave way to dictation. And the panel of agency CEOs charged with ensuring the synergy of the structure failed to make that happen. The Power of One eventually became the power of none.

Two agency-wide meetings at Devon Direct testified to Ron Greene's state of mind under all this Euro pressure. He invited the staff to air their concerns to him so he might fully understand their thoughts on how to move forward and solve problems that were affecting morale. The staff opened up, vented their grievances and proposed remedies for making their lives more sane.

Following that session, Ron called management to a closed-door meeting at which he railed on about the complaints he had heard and how we managers were to blame for these attitudes because we had lost our control over the staff. I went back to my office and shook my head in disbelief.

Then even more telling was the speech he made to the agency on October 20, 2000 . . . a year after Devon Direct joined Euro RSCG. It was peppered with a vehement denunciation of the status quo—totally devoid of his usual reverence and respect for the dedicated employees who had taken the agency to the top of Direct Marketing.

He talked of a new, flatter, more streamlined organizational structure for the company, necessitated by the lack of a sense of excitement and groundbreaking initiatives. He said: "to be successful we will need to get out from under the bureaucracy we have grown into and which has been stifling us." He told the employees that they must make a commitment to working longer and harder, that they should not watch the clock and expect to go home at the end of the workday. He also told them if they couldn't exercise more self-discipline and self-motivation, they would not be successful or happy in this new structure.

What he said next convinced me that the Ron Greene I had known no longer existed.

"If the organization I've described to you is not for you, if it is not a commitment you want to make, if the demands and expectations are beyond what you choose to embrace in your professional life, you should have a conversation with your supervisor." Implying if you don't like it, leave.

Do you talk this way to employees who have proved their value over and over again and who had always put in whatever time was necessary to get the job done? I think not. It was a demoralizing moment. Plus, what happened to me in this realignment shocked the agency. Yet attempts to reverse this decision fell on deaf ears and further depressed morale.

CHAPTER 8

DISMANTLING THE BUREAUCRACY

The linchpin to the new structure was to remove all writers, with the exception of the top-level Copy Creative Directors, from my supervision and put them under Ron's brother Brian. Most of the staff, particularly the writers, wondered why Ron would do such a thing. Brian, nice guy (a veneer to some) was completely without creative credentials. The employees concluded that Ron felt he had to give Brian something to do. A travesty, they thought, since I was considered to be the most disciplined and effective manager in the agency while Brian was looked upon by many in the company as a case of family favoritism. To say the least, my writers were nonplused. They had lost me as their advocate in management on matters of career advancement, compensation and recognition. With me, they knew their performance reviews would be completed on schedule instead of months late, as with other agency supervisors, including Ron Greene. In fact, Ron and brother Brian were the biggest delinquents. After the writers were removed from my supervision, on-time performance reviews became a low priority. Another morale depressant.

Despite the prevailing view that this new structure was the wrong way to go, Ron saw it as breaking out of the organizational boxes and contributing to our ability to act and think globally. Since he stubbornly refused to rethink this action, I decided to live with it and continue to offer my best. Other aspects of the reorganization were simply window dressing. And the whole thing accomplished nothing but a deepening gloom over where we were heading.

Ron's next move was equally bewildering. He requested from each member of management a document listing what they had done for the agency. This was my submission:

In the early years of my employment, and even beyond in guiding and managing creative for such clients as Sprint, Bell Atlantic, MCI, ADT, British Telecom, etc, I worked late into the night on a daily basis to help grow our company. Not because I was ordered to do so, but because I was excited, highly motivated and amply rewarded. You often used to say that you wanted me to have whatever I needed to make my life more sane. I still come to work early in the morning and seldom take a lunch hour.

I worked for many years to build one of the toughest, most productive and marketing smart copy departments in direct response advertising. I welded that department into a functioning team—and devoted my efforts toward ensuring that it would always be worthy of your confidence. I have also been instrumental in widening the department's interactive capabilities.

I have won the respect of every department in the company, contributed continually to the solution of complex client-related problems, been part of the heart and soul of what was an enviable culture and strongly influenced the quality and creativity of the Art Department . . . ensuring the compatibility of art and copy.

As to listing on paper what else I've done for the company—it's already on paper, defined by your own words in every performance appraisal you have completed for me year after year, in the highest ratings you have given me time after time, and in the accolades you gave me on the occasion of my 10th anniversary . . . one of those comments being that you could not have built the company without me. I have never forgotten the satisfaction I felt when I heard you say that.

I am not a bureaucrat. I am not boxed in by position and title. I will do whatever you need me to do and spend whatever time it takes to do it. But I cannot guarantee—in these later years of my life—that I will turn my back on the need to balance my worklife responsibilities with the requirement to be a devoted husband and take time to enjoy the rewards of a long and productive life.

On redefining my position according to your vision of a different kind of company, I will be whatever you want me to be. I can administer teams of designers and copywriters in a tighter resource framework. I can write copy myself. I can take a stronger role in marketing. I can be some kind of agency wide problem-solving administrator. To an extent, I do all these things already . . . and I would be pleased to work out the specifics with you when the "new agency" you propose is ready to be implemented.

So what was Ron's response to this memo? None! I did ask him at a later date if he agreed with everything I had said in this document. His answer: "yes, absolutely." Did he ever meet with me to work out the specifics of making this new structure viable? Absolutely not! I will never fathom his motive in asking management to deliver these defensive epistles. How could a CEO not be cognizant of what each of his direct reports had done or not done for the company? Most of all, I will never understand his downgrading of my leadership position, especially in light of performance appraisals similar to the following in every one of my 16 plus years.

EXEMPT PERFORMANCE APPRAISAL

Employee Name:	Allen Stone
Employee Title:	VP Creative Director
Department Name:	Copy
Hire Date:	2/26/87
Performance Review Period:	12/11/95-12/11/96

Use the following rating scale for each category listed:

5—Substantially exceeds position requirements
4—Exceeds position requirements
3—Attains position requirements
2—Almost attains position requirements
1—Substantially fails to attain position requirements

Evaluation of overall performance

Rating: 5

Comments: Allen is responsible for the management of the Copy Department, including the copy requirements for all clients, the development of creative talent, idea generation, and the ongoing requirements of the agency's Creative Process.

Individual assessment factors

A) Job Knowledge

Rating: 5

Strengths: An advertising marketing pro with incredible depth and understanding for the creative needs of the agency and our clients. A true problem-solver whose creative abilities contribute throughout our company, giving shape, substance, style, and quality to our entire work output.

B) Judgement and Decisions

Rating: 5

Strengths: Very strategic marketing creative problem-solver. Management experience gives Allen ability to anticipate problems and issues before they occur and provide solutions within budget and staff parameters. Very effective in providing balanced viewpoint across departments.

C) Plan and Organize

Rating: 5

Strengths: Highly organized with strong logistical and administrative/business skills. Allen's management gives the agency the ability to deliver consistent/on-time performance.

D) Management of Resources

Rating: 5

Strengths: Gets true and efficient productivity from staff. Continues to mentor talent and has built a very effective departmental management team.

E) Leadership

Rating: 5

Strengths: Performs and contributes at the highest level of the agency. Allen is sought out by other top-level managers to help contribute to all areas of the company. Provides substantive contributions to Management Committee, and I depend upon Allen to represent the agency with clients, prospects and industry trade associations.

F) Communication

Rating: 5

Strengths: The best! Commanding presentation style. Always incredibly prepared.

Other relevant assessments

Allen is continuing to push for highest creative performance from his staff, as well as from the Art Department. He is continuing to develop his team for both management and creative perspectives

I continue to rely upon Allen's judgement and insight on a wide range of issues and look to Allen as one of the key leaders of the company.

Reviewer: Ron Greene   Date: 12/20/96

Considering the above and down-the-line 5 ratings, I was dumbfounded when Ron emasculated my department and reasoned that it would help take us out of our doldrums. It simply didn't make any sense. And it did not, in any measure, accomplish his purpose.

Our depressed condition reached a point whereby Devon's only big-budget anchor client was Nextel, and that business showed signs of withering on the vine. Increasingly, Nextel put us in the position of competing with other agencies for work—despite the fact that most of the times they engaged in this practice, our ideas beat out those of the competing agencies. New marketing major-domos with their own favorite agencies joined the wireless provider. Faster, better, cheaper became the order of the day. Projects diminished precipitously and it was apparent that we were being pushed aside. This despite years of producing promotional vehicles that fared well in the marketplace, gave this client a higher profile offline as well as online and maximized Nextel's investment in Direct Response advertising.

Our people had given blood to this client. Their work had garnered 36 prestigious industry awards in 3 years. What they got in return as time went by was nothing short of shabby. Adding to that, "faster, better, cheaper" became the pervasive clarion call in advertising.

CHAPTER 9

FASTER, BETTER, CHEAPER

For Devon Direct and other Euro RSCG agencies this client-induced mandate, in itself, became a roadblock to realization of Bob Schmetterer's Creative Business Ideas. Even before 9/11 and the sagging economy, clients were pressing agencies to accelerate the completion of their advertising, to turn out projects that were bigger winners in the marketplace and to do it all for less. If clients could get another agency to work cheaper—out you go.

At the same time, agencies were paying more for goods and services. Paper costs were going up. Production costs were increasing. Medical expenditures for employee coverage were skyrocketing. Agency travel expenses were on the rise. Merit salary increases and annual bonuses were taking a toll. New business acquisition expenses were escalating. And notably, the cost of postage and changing post office regulations—a huge factor in high-volume Direct Marketing—were up sharply. There was no way to pass all this on to clients. So profit margins were being strangled at a time when acquiring new clients to pay the bills was becoming more difficult.

"Faster, better, cheaper" meant agencies had to fight harder to maintain the quality of their advertising. They developed formats with longer shelf life, sought savings on paper stocks, opened production contracts to competitive bidding, charged employees more for their medical plans, cut back on air travel, developed more stringent salary control programs, pared down bonuses, put a hold on additional resources . . . and penny-pinched wherever they could.

Most of all, clients wanted a higher response rate in the marketplace. They were no longer satisfied with the direct marketing benchmark of 1% to 5% of the number of promotions mailed out. Agencies bent every effort to bring clients a better return on their investment. There were times when we achieved response rates as high as 40%, like in the case of British Telecom. But even when you brought in a stronger response, it didn't always ensure client longevity. When you hit the mark, you were a hero. When you missed the mark, it was "what have you done for me lately?"

Now we were into the new century and the outlook continued to be bleak—made worse by 9/11 and the economic malaise. Client attrition at Devon Direct was seriously threatening the agency's financial health. Companies like Sprint, MCI, Bell Atlantic, British Telecom, ADT, J.I. Case, Fleet, GMAC, Kenwood, VeriSign and IBM were long gone. So were the Devon Direct offices in New York, London and California.

In addition, we seemed to be losing out in our ability to attract RFIs and RFPs. An RFI is a Request For Information from a prospective client. An RFP is a Request For Proposal. RFPs are invitations from a company to agencies thought to be the right fit to compete in-person for the client's advertising business. The agencies chosen to receive RFIs and RFPs are usually identified by specialized consultants retained by clients.

Why was it, then, that many of these consultants representing big-budget clients looking for an agency did not seem to know we existed? As big as we were and as strong a track record as we established, our PR in this respect was paltry. We were inept at marketing ourselves. Our efforts at acquiring the kind of clients who could keep us alive and growing were anemic. We were not "kicking ass," an expression advertising folk find useful in describing a high level of success . . . whether in returning from a triumphant RFP performance, winning a new client or scoring a marketplace hit for an existing client.

The latter was becoming an increasingly skull-cracking mission because faster, better, cheaper coincided with the fact that the advertising community could no longer rely on recycling past strategies. Far-reaching changes were emerging in consumer behavior and these marketplace realities were altering the business environment and calling for a radical reconsideration in the way agencies act on behalf of their clients.

Agencies would have to acquire sharper insights into consumer attitudes and demonstrate an increased sensitivity to a dramatically changed world.

To do this, agencies had to divest themselves of worn out, cliched attitudes, think in new ways and employ new research tools.

Pursuing that mission, our parent Euro RSCG coined a new word to label the increasingly discerning consumer: *The Prosumer.* Proactive and technologically adept, prosumers—according to Euro—want to know they've made the right choices. They want more products to choose from. They are information-hungry. They need to know everything about a brand, the people behind it and especially how it will impact their everyday lives. They are acquiring a sophistication that leads them to feel victimized and manipulated by advertising.

With all this in mind, agencies are heightening their dependency on new research that is able to hone in on these changing marketplace conditions and give rise to powerful new ideas and breakthrough advertising solutions. They are engaged in an ongoing analysis of current and future trends that could significantly impact the way people live and work. They are seeking new strategies to differentiate products for the intended audience.

And recognizing that happy customers are the best source for incremental revenue, ad agencies are pursuing new approaches at building brand loyalty for their clients.

A major research tool agencies subscribe to in their efforts at understanding the evolving marketplace as well as changing consumer behavior is the universally respected and scholarly Yankelovich report.

I'm reminded of the winning tagline an advertising agency genius came up with for Smucker's preserves that reads: "With a name like Smucker's, it has to be good."

With a name like Yankelovich the research better be good . . . and it is!

According to Yankelovich research,* "It's no surprise that consumers demonstrate a love-hate relationship with advertising. Often it's seen as an intrusion, especially on the Internet where a growing majority of consumers find advertising to be a disappointing aspect of their online experience."

Yankelovich says marketers need to make sure they communicate with clarity so consumers can feel comfortable about their activity in the marketplace. The point being: "In this economy a lack of credible information will not instill the confidence they need to invest in a product or service."

As an example, Yankelovich cites financial services where the research shows that clarity is lacking, with 4 in 10 consumers saying they're confused about how to invest their money.

No surprise either is the Yankelovich finding that friends and family are particularly influential when it comes to forming opinions about new products or services. And that men are more likely to say it's worth the effort to spend time researching a product before buying.

---

* Yankelovich MONITOR 2003

Yankelovich concludes that one of the biggest challenges marketers face during these troubled times is "finding the right voice and environment for communicating with consumers."

Through the years, Yankelovich and other Euro-supplied research devices served as useful instruments of strategic trendspotting for the marketing people at Devon Direct. We utilized such vital aides as:

White Papers—analyses of current and future trends that significantly impact the way people live and work.

Five Points Process™—five specific steps to help planners ask the right questions, at precisely the right stage in the marketing process.

Marketing Architecture—A map of the consumer's experience with a brand, to coordinate marketing more efficiently and effectively.

Agency War Rooms—Everything that everyone from every discipline has come to know or suspect in a client's business.

Momentum Polling—a way to monitor shifts in consumer perceptions of brands and keep a close watch on the ebb and flow of public opinion.

CHAPTER 10

CHANGING COLORS

As our black ink threatened to turn red, the preoccupation aimed at understanding the evolving consumer environment took a back seat to figuring out how to rescue the agency from the abyss.

Leaders are supposed to *lead*, but Ron continued to back off from dealing with the problems. The employees talked amongst themselves, wondering why he wouldn't DO SOMETHING! "Jeez, make a decision, any decision," they would say. At least people would respect him for trying, instead of turning a blind eye to what was happening. But Ron was playing out his time. The end of his contract with Euro was near. He knew he would soon go out with millions. So, it's reasonable to ask, why should he do anything? He probably had long since concluded that there was nothing he could do to halt the downward spiral.

Attention focused on the actions of Finance Director Mark Mandia.

Though affable, capable and respected, he had little sensitivity to the motivational needs of our employees. But, unlike Ron, Mark did not shy away from making decisions.

He erased discretionary bonuses in favor of an incentive plan based on the billable hours of each employee and each was given a billable mandate. Thus, employees were made responsible for increasing their client billable hours at a time when business was on the slide. I asked how the agency could commit the staff to push up their billings when the work was going down—even as the company could not deliver on its part of the incentive plan to acquire clients who would provide the work and make higher billings possible. "Mark" I said, "isn't this a contradiction in terms, an oxymoron? How can you have one without the other?" He was not open to reason. But he was one of my consistent supporters in the management structure, so rather than create enmity, I backed off.

However, who could blame Mark Mandia for sticking to his guns? Like Ron Greene, he was chafing under the need to put profit dollars into the Euro coffers. And Euro, for its part, was pressing to prop up its parent Havas as the French communications giant fought to cauterize its own financial bleeding.

Bent on meeting our Euro obligations, and faced with the fact that the level of workload and revenue was out of kilter with the level of staffing, Mark Mandia took to examining each department and issuing orders for downsizing.

We lost many of the veteran employees and top professionals who numbered among the best in the advertising business . . . people we had labored long and hard to find. I will never forget the hurt I felt when I called in Copy Creative Director Elliot Simmons to inform him that his days at Devon were finished. He had been with me for 15 years and was as clever and zany a writer as I've ever encountered. The following bears testimony to that. When our frustrating relationship with Kenwood Sterio Systems ended, Elliot—the writer assigned to the business—authored this parody satirizing the pain and suffering he and his fellow Devonites endured as they tried to satisfy the Kenwood consultant (Geheran) forced on the agency, and others at the client (Alluraland) charged with supervising and approving the work.

Though you may not comprehend all the insider language in Elliot's parody, you will get the point and likely empathize with the sigh of relief that went up when this client walked away from us.

THE GEHERAN AND THE DEVONITES
A biblical fable by Elliot Simmons

So it came to pass . . . That the Geheran with his beloved Sharmmon, sent by the Lord Richter, led the Devonites out of the house of bondage, out of their land of Berwyn toward the light of Alluraland.

After many days travel, the multitude stopped to rest in the valley next to Mount Kenwood. And the Geheran went up the mountain. And spake, "I submit that when I return I shall have all the answers . . . the copy . . . the design . . . the art and the Web site for Alluraland. Till my return my beloved Sharmmon the Squeezeable and my lackey, the good and faithful Arvin Itis, will keep me in touch from my remote location."

But the Geheran was away for many, many days. And the Devonites grew restless. They started to create their own DM packages and Web site for Alluraland.

Ye did they write copy . . . Ye did they design packages . . . And hither did they dare to make site maps and Web packages.

And they did revel in the joy of music and Alluraland. And they forgot about the Geheran. They created for themselves. And a cheer went up from among the Devonites shouting, "Verily we have done some damn fine work!"

But their glee was short lived. For the Geheran returned from Mount Kenwood after reviewing the work of the Devonites and carrying two giant tablets with many notes and revelations. And he spake unto the children of Devon Direct, "I have seen what thee have created. And it was good—verily for the first try. But basically, it ateth shit!"

He then went on and on, and on, and on, and on saying, "I have brought you a few hundreth pageth of noteth. The basicth of which are these Ten Commandments of Advertising which you will find in my power point presentation. And they are good, verily, verily, verily good."

The Ten Commandments of Advertising
(Carved in stone by the Geheran)

1. Thou shalt not use redundant, superfluous, elongated over-rated hyperbole unless it can be quoted from a third party or from the mouth of the Geheran.

2. Thou shalt remember the Chesky and keep it holy.

3. Thou shalt have no other consultants before thee.

4. Thou shalt keep thy DM piece clean and not soil it with an offer.

5. Thou shalt not display the Allura speakers or your private parts with the screen or your pants off.

6. Thou shalt not place the Allura speakers on top of, or inside a fireplace unless listening to hot music.

7. Thou shalt not lead the reader to any conclusion, verily let them make their own damn decision.

8. Thou shalt not call the InView Controller a remote.

9. Thou shalt not take the name of the Geheran in vain.

10. Thou shalt honor the name of Kenwood and the Geheran from this day forward.

And when the Geheran had finished, the Devonites looked up in awe. Not at the Geheran, however. They were moved to tears by the Devon Prophets Dessi, O'Brien, Rowinski, Richardson, Moore, Breen and Simmons as they pushed a huge boulder over a ledge that fell on the Geheran and crushed the fucker flat.

And when they saw what they had done, the Prophets stood on the top of Mount Kenwood and shouted, "Party Time!"

And so it was written.

And so it was done.

Elliot Simmons. He was a gem. And so was Vice President/Art Creative Director Peter Richardson, the next under my supervision to go. Peter served Devon with distinction. He was an outstanding Direct Response creative resource. I had known Peter from our days together at the Franklin Mint and he was the first designer I hired to help me build one of the most capable art departments in advertising. Peter and the artists who worked with him created masterful promotions for Sprint, Bell Atlantic, Advanta, Fleet Financial and many other frontline Devon clients. Invariably, Peter was the choice of our marketers to present creative work at client meetings. He knew how to talk to clients, how to point out the strengths of the work, and how to win client approval.

Elliot and Peter were only two of the many veteran employees—some with 10 to15 years of service and unflinching loyalty—put out on the street with little hope of equaling the positions and incomes they enjoyed at Devon Direct. Several of the writers and designers turned to freelancing and today are continuing to produce superior advertising for clients fortunate to have them aboard.

In our glory days, we employed close to 200 people. That would scale down to less than 40 before the end became inevitable. And among those dismissed by the company or who saw the gathering dark clouds and left were several of the "new breed" designers and writers who had become masters of Web technology and wizards in maximizing the value of interactive applications for companies who sought to drive sales through the power of the Internet.

CHAPTER II

TALENT FOR THE TIMES

These online creative people not only understood the technological complexity involved in writing and designing entire Web sites, but also how to work magic with the many new and exciting interactive functions that were coming into play almost every day. They put Devon Direct a giant step ahead in the development of sophisticated Internet strategies and ran the gauntlet in bringing creativity together with online technology.

Can you imagine the brainpower and digital dexterity necessary to absorb and create applications like the following:*

Banner—A graphic that appears on a Web page that is usually hyperlinked to an advertiser's Web site. May appear in a variety of formats and include animation.

---

*   Source: AdGlossary
     Online advertising glossary
     http://www.adglossary.com

Hyperlink—An HTML code, when clicked on, redirects ones browser to the advertiser's Web page for further product information.

HTML—Computer programming language that helps control the format of a document's content and design on the Web.

Interstitial—An intrusive, often animated, type of ad that appears on a Web page without being requested by the visitor.

Superstitial™—Attractive to advertisers because it permits a larger and more interactive ad than a banner. Since they pre-load in the background, they are not as annoying as Interstitials or Pop-Ups.

Pop Up—A type of obtrusive, high-visibility advertisement automatically displayed on a Web page that is often annoying to visitors.

Skyscraper Ads—Named for their tall, skinny height. Because of their greater surface area, advertisers can convey more of a message visually, textually, or both.

Rich Media—A type of technology that can include more complex graphics as well as audio or video within the ad and often enables users to interact with the advertisement . . . like playing games, making selections and entering information. All without leaving the Web site.

GIF—Sequences of images combined to create animated banners on Web pages.

Java—programming language that enables developers to write software on one platform and run it on another. Software platforms include Windows and Unix.

Shoshkeles™—named for the daughter of their creator, this application features floating graphics that incorporate sound and move across an entire Web page instead of residing in a fixed location. They get the vote for the latest "cool" factor.

Sponsorships—Usually built to suit the advertiser, sponsorship packages allow dominance of a Web page or section of a Web site.

Text Boxes—They provide more space in which to communicate a message. Heavy borders and contrasting colors help improve response rates.

These are only a few of the applications online writers and designers must comprehend in this age of the Internet. Hardly a day passes without something new to learn. There are an increasing number of advertising agencies who are restricting their output to Web-based advertising and swallowing up these "new breed" practitioners. There are also an increasing number of businesses that are calling on these agencies to market their products and services on the Web . . . the ultimate direct marketing channel.

It is a sin and a shame that Devon Direct's leadership and pioneering achievements in this realm fell victim to the agency's demise.

In the spring of 2003, it was apparent that Euro RSCG Devon Direct was in its death throes, and that Euro would have to make its peace with the agency's irreversible illness.

I put down a plan for ending my career. I saw no other option after what Ron Greene had revealed to management at a meeting a few weeks earlier.

The agency would be merged with one of Euro's more stable companies. "Merged" was the word Ron used. Had he been leveling with us, the word should have been "absorbed."

We had questions:

"Would we keep our name?"

"I don't know."

"Will we be moved to New York?"

"I don't know."

"When will this happen?"

"Probably soon."

We were advised not to say anything to the agency until more was known. We didn't have to say anything. The employees had already concluded that the situation had reached a point where Euro would have no choice but to step in.

Then, no job would be safe, mine especially. What would they want with a high-priced vice president? And what would I come out with if I waited till after a Euro takeover?

I discussed the matter behind closed doors with Mark Mandia. We agreed on a financial arrangement which he submitted to Ron and which would allow me to leave with dignity. Ron gave his approval and insisted on a party. His remarks at that luncheon on April 22, 2003—my final day—were vintage Ron Greene. Permit me to share them.

"It would be impossible to encapsulate all that Allen has contributed to Devon Direct during the past 16 years in anything close to a few words. Perhaps only he, copywriter extraordinaire that he is, could do such an endeavor justice.

His credo Make Every Word Sell, which has guided the development of copy at Devon Direct since its earliest days, is the only derivative phrase with which Allen has ever been associated. It derives from Strunk & White's Elements of Style—I believe one of Allen's bibles— and the original is Make Every Word Tell. So rather than attempt to come up with something that would pass Allen's formidable blue pencil, I will go with Strunk & White.

When it comes to Allen and what he has meant to Devon Direct, these are the words that tell:

OUR FIRST AND ONLY COPY CHIEF

ARCHITECT OF CREATIVE EXCELLENCE

MANAGER OF THE CREATIVE PROCESS

MENTOR OF CREATIVE TALENT

ADVOCATE FOR HIS STAFF

CHAMPION OF TEAMWORK AND COMMUNICATION

LOYAL . . . DEDICATED . . . AND DEVOTED TO ALL THAT DEVON DIRECT HAS EVER ASPIRED TO BE.

And, LEGACY—for that is what Allen leaves us with . . . the professionalism and standards that bear his signature will continue to guide our creative efforts.

And these words tell too, maybe most of all:

ALLEN, WE WILL MISS YOU.

The words we don't have are the ones that could possibly thank you enough for your years and years of service, and the 1000% you gave us in each and every one of those years, each and every day.

Allen, we offer a toast to you—celebrating your years at Devon Direct and celebrating all that you have planned for the next chapter in your life. May your future be as rich as the 16 years you have shared with us."

These attaboys from this man who had provided me with opportunities I never dreamed possible will remain with me for the rest of my days. For at the end of a long career, there is nothing more meaningful than being recognized as a dedicated professional who never gave less than the best. For personal self-esteem, this is the reward that carries an unparalleled sense of satisfaction. And even with the ill-conceived notions and actions attributed to Ron Greene in this book, I will always value the years I was privileged to serve him. His capabilities are undeniable, his character is unassailable.

Soon after my exit, Ron sent an email to the agency announcing his own departure. Mark Mandia was next, leaving the company leaderless. Euro overseers came down to our Berwyn, Pennsylvania offices from New York. Further layoffs and resignations ensued. The staff became a skeleton of what it had been in the glory days and our beautiful facility, which once occupied two floors of a prestigious corporate center in suburban Philadelphia, was stripped down to a corner of the building.

The terminal indignity: It was the autumn of 2003. Devon Direct, struggling to survive, was in danger of losing its identity. As this book went to press, Euro RSCG was deciding whether to rename the company, shut the doors altogether, or absorb the remains of what had been one of America's first-ranking Direct Response advertising agencies. Thus taking an industry leader to the brink of mortality and . . .

The Death Of Success.

EPILOGUE

FACING THE FACTS

E verything Devon Direct had been, it was no more. The great people I was privileged to work with became shadows from the past. But I think all would agree that we had been at the right place at the right time. We had grown as professionals and benefited from the pursuit of perfection. We had experienced the high that comes with success, unfortunately also the low that accompanies the death of success.

Two funky oil paintings from our agency cafe, which had always brought a smile to my face, were presented to me on the day of my departure. They hang on my kitchen wall and every morning, when I have coffee prior to taking my daily walk, they remind me of my 16 halcyon years at a wonderful company whose epitaph should read: *We did it so right for so long.*

As to the advertising industry itself, the negatives I've pointed to in this book are not meant to upstage the positives. Its genius resides in the incredible skills of its people. It offers creative satisfaction and career growth to all who can bear up under its exacting demands. Advertising entertains while it informs. It enables companies to prosper and enhances their ability to enrich their employees. It acquaints us with the products and services that can make a difference in our lives. Without advertising, how would we make sense of what a product is all about and whether or not we should buy it? There is no need for schooling to understand that where consumer spending goes, so goes the economy—particularly in the absence of other cushioning factors, such as a favorable trade balance. Advertising is the stimulus that drives and strengthens our economic engine. And "conspicuous consumption"—a pejorative often used by other countries to disparage American values—is, in reality, what makes our economy work.

This is not to simplistically postulate that advertising is the be-all and end-all of keeping the wheels of self-sufficiency turning. But there's no getting away from the fact that it is a basic and necessary causal factor in maintaining our economic existence . . . for which it receives only the barest of credit.

Peering into the crystal ball, here are the heralds of the future. In this era of evolving marketplace attitudes, the advertising industry will encounter heavy pressure to measure up to the task of answering the needs of increasingly skeptical and sophisticated consumers. It will be under the gun to tame its excesses, find new and different ways to serve its clients and approach its target audiences—but that will happen only if the public exercises *its* responsibility to be the arbiter of integrity.

This watchdog role obligates all of us to be on alert for exaggerated claims, half-truths and advertising seduction. As you strive to satisfy your needs for goods and services, stick to doing business with the brands you trust. Be careful of the fine print. Watch out for chicanery on the Web. Pay attention to the privacy statements you receive from companies. Above all, be wary of providing credit card information that could ensnare you into unwanted and repeat purchases as well as membership in clubs that could cost you money and put you through a quagmire of frustration in attempting to get off their computers.

As always, it's buyer beware and all that glitters is not gold.

In saying that, I'm reminded of Vance Packard's best-selling *The Hidden Persuaders,* published in 1957. It revealed the psychological machinations used by advertisers to get inside consumers' brains. He opened up on marketers, accusing them of employing all manner of deceptions to manipulate the buying public. Even today, there is an intuitive feeling that advertisers are liars and ruthless in exploiting consumers. In 1964, Packard authored *The Naked Society,* compounding his earlier accusations in a discussion about the techniques corporations use to gather personal information about citizens.

Whatever the excesses, It was not easy to walk away from this exciting and high-energy profession. Drudgery notwithstanding, the day is fast and even fun in an ad agency. Boredom is unknown. You're busier than the proverbial "one-arm paper hanger." Talent is respected and rewarded. Brainpower is needed and expected. What you're able to do today, you're better at tomorrow. Victories are celebrated. Defeats are a learning curve.

As we noted at the outset . . . there's no business like the advertising business, and no people like advertising people.

Finally, a personal postscript: It is addressed to those who desire to open up a career opportunity in advertising or, for that matter, any profession. From my experience, there are three simple requisites. Someone needs to be interested in you. That someone needs to have a position for which they think you are qualified. And when you attain that position, you need to prove they were right.

Now, turn to the back cover, and see if you don't smile too.

www.ingramcontent.com/pod-product-compliance
Lightning Source LLC
Chambersburg PA
CBHW031952190326
41519CB00007B/769